MW00815628

A Couple,
Still

"[I] feel that I have vicariously walked with Frances through an experience that reaches to the depth of human life – a search for the meaning of 'being.' It is a personal and intimate story that I believe can bring healing grace to thousands of people who are trying to find their way through one of life's most painful experiences. It is a book which I wish I could have had – and would like to have now – to give to many, many people with whom I have stood when they were facing the experience about which Frances has so eloquently written."

—*W. Burkett Raper, President Emeritus, Mount Olive College*

"I read *A Couple Still* with a deep sense of privilege. Frances L. Cooke has allowed the reader access to the dark soul of her grief and beyond to the sunlight of her recovery. When told it was a narrative of that journey I had expected something much different—a how-to manual in the vein of those that her beloved Howard prized so highly. Although the nuts and bolts of the practical matters that must be dealt with in the aftermath of the death of a spouse are touched on with clarity, other sources will need to be consulted for their details. This is a roller coaster ride of the emotions with gut wrenching twists and turns. Some will need to read in small doses with a box of tissues at hand. All will profit from this riveting and uplifting journey through grief."

—*Clyde Smith,*
Deputy Secretary of State (retired), State of North Carolina

"The biographer, Thomas Carlyle, understood the difficulty of the art and once observed, 'A well written life is almost as rare as a well spent one.' Frances Cooke has succeeded here in constructing a mosaic from a myriad of colored fragments that came out of the loss of her beloved husband, Howard. She has created out of numerous details, a comprehensive and unified portrait of one person's bout with grief. This book is a faithful rendering that comes out of an exemplary Christian life and marriage. It reminds me of the poet's phrase that "the light, returning, shall give back the golden hours."

—*Dr. Mark T. White, Pastor*
Bethlehem Baptist Church, Knightdale, NC

"The personal reflections in this love story provide lessons for each person who has experienced, or will in the future experience, loss of a spouse or cherished friend. The most significant gift to this reader was how the author accepted that her deceased spouse continues to be a part of her life. It is also exciting as to how God led this couple to accept the difficult experiences leading up to Howard's death as spiritual growth moments as well as further development of their deep love for each other."

—Edwin S. Coates,
Executive Director (Retired)
North Carolina Baptist Foundation, Inc., (1972-97)

"What a wonderful testimony! As a fellow traveler for less than a year, I think I have delineated several perennial questions that, although common to those who have lost a spouse, must be addressed uniquely by each person on this journey. In this book, and in a way that is most helpful to us fellow travelers, Frances has articulated exceptionally well how she has faced those questions, has answered some of them, and continues to manage the others. I say manage since I am increasingly doubtful that all of these questions have answers in this life, and that managing must become woven into the fabric of daily living. I can only imagine the quantity and, more to the point, the grueling quality of hours she has spent in order to bring this resource to us. This is not another "cookbook approach," but rather a "Cooke book" approach to responding to a major problem. I am most grateful that she tenaciously dedicated her time to the task for the edification of all who will read it."

—John F. Freeman, Jr., Lecturer
Graphics Communication Department of
Mathematics, Science and Technology Education
North Carolina State University

Frances and Howard in 1944, just after their marriage

A Couple, Still

A Personal Journey To Recovery and Independence After Bereavement

FRANCES L. COOKE

AVENTURA PRESS
Eynon, PA

To Sara and Jack-
whose "peace of God"
message profoundly
touched me -

Frances L. Cooke

Cover and interior design by Lee Sebastiani & Lori Sebastiani, Avventura Press
Photos: Frances L. Cooke

Copyright © 2006 by Frances L. Cooke. All rights reserved.
Previously published as Recovery: A Personal Journey

Library of Congress Control Number: 2007942117

ISBN-13: 978-0-9761553-1-7

Published by
Avventura Press
133 Handley St.
Eynon PA 18403-1305
570-876-5817
www.avventurapress.com

1st printing January, 2008
Printed in the United States of America

Foreward

Some years ago, Dr. Dale H. Gramley, president of Salem—a women's college in Winston-Salem, North Carolina—addressed a commencement audience, saying, "You must all prepare for your own inevitable solitude." The words "inevitable solitude" may have merely skimmed the surface of understanding in the minds of the youthful graduates; however, as women grow older and contemplate their tomorrows, the phrase may predict more realistically the longevity statistics of gender, the empty nests, the financial stability or lack thereof, the loneliness, and so on.

The author of this memoir was as prepared as any independent female executive, mother, grandmother, churchwoman would be. In the fourteen months of her husband's life following the numbing diagnosis of terminal illness, Frances Cooke gave herself the freedom and faith to face an unknown world. She and her husband, Howard, did not evade the inevitable. Together they talked comfortably, planned thoroughly, laughed, cried, and strengthened their spiritual resolve. Perhaps, however, Frances was not so well prepared for the myriad routine responsibilities that Howard had always assumed nevertheless, she staunchly faced them—sometimes in anger, usually in frustration, oftentimes in tears, but always with determination.

As the hours and days and months and years pass, the grief doesn't; rather, it adopts a new character, which this writer expresses in words and in ways that lift her readers from empathetic sadness to emotional healing, from darkness to light. Particularly in chapter 13—the author's canon of God's omnipresence in the lives of His twenty-first century disciples—the reader takes another bold step in the recovery from his or her own grief.

In two recent successive years, Frances Cooke traveled to China, where she taught English to Chinese teachers and where she visited a university that had housed Howard and other United States servicemen in World War II. Those experiences seemed to escort her into her new life with hope and, yes, joy. This memoir does the same for her readers.

Carolyn C. Robinson
Director of Alumni Affairs (retired) and Historian
Meredith College, Raleigh, North Carolina

PREFACE

Writers must, by nature, be egotistical people. To even imagine that someone wishes to read what they write is purest egotism. Aware of that fact, this is written especially for my children and grandchildren. Because of our relationship, because of the subject matter, and, out of simple curiosity they will probably give at least a casual examination to what I have written. If, in the meantime, others express interest in reading my thoughts on the most difficult period of my life, I will have accomplished my goal.

The traumatic months of my husband's illness and death cast grief on our family, especially on me. The months have also been a period of maturing in faith. My own spiritual growth has made me much more sensitive to the life experiences of others. I have been there myself.

This one thing I know: recovery is tentative and, as with physical trauma, will be affected by many factors. There are the first cautious signs when one deals with the routine of daily living. And then there is the broadside when you realize you will never fully recover, that never will life be as it was, and your passage to full recovery will continue forever.

To my friends, my family, especially my daughters and their families, and to anyone who experiences grief from the loss of a loved one, I share my heart. There is no attempt to present a clinical analysis of grief, about which I know absolutely nothing. This has become a memoir of my slow crawl through recovery, my purely personal feelings, unique to me. Perhaps they are also experienced by others, and hence are not at all unique! It is my hope that their telling may be helpful where needed, just as their writing has been therapeutic for me.

FLC
February 5, 2005

Howard's home in Amherst, Massachusetts

Chapter 1

An Introduction to Grief

It has now been three months since Howard died. No— as this is being written it has been three years! That's the way grief is. Some days it is so raw and intense, it must have just happened. Then weeks may pass when one deals with life as it comes and time passes normally.

When I retired in 1988 from The North Carolina Baptist Foundation, following thirty-two years of work as a career with the local church, the Baptist Association and the Foundation, there were four things I promised myself I would do just for me: learn to play golf, learn how to hook rugs the old-fashioned way as my grandmother did it, practice the piano until I recovered my ability to play well enough to give me personal pleasure, and finally, to write my book. Retirement did not happen the way I planned!

First, Howard and I were immediately required to make numerous trips to care for his ailing aunt and uncle in Massachusetts, Aunt Marjorie and Harvey. One year we made nine trips from North Carolina to Amherst! Then my father became ill with Alzheimer-like dementia, and our attention was turned to him and to Mother who was caring for him. Howard and I were the persons who finally made the emergency decision that Dad required more help than the family could give. Mother needed protection as he became more angry and volatile in his actions toward her, something which was completely uncharacteristic for him. We, with Mother and brother Bill, took control and committed Dad involuntarily to Dorothea Dix Hospital, the state mental facility. There, he received attention from doctors who were trained in the illness he suffered. They were able, also, to give assistance to the family, both in guidance for us and in giving Dad the care he needed so that Mother was able to return him to their home. Following his death in February 1992, we turned our attention again to the needs calling us in Massachusetts, and were there when both Harvey and Aunt Marjorie died within six days of each other in October 1992.

In the meantime, I did learn how to hook rugs. Golf and piano practice are still on the back burner. And my book is not to be the kind I anticipated writing. In my closet are stacks of scripts of Sunday School lessons prepared for radio and television, which I taught for the Sunday School and communications departments of the Baptist State Convention over a period of nearly twelve years. It had been my intention and desire to compile the anecdotes in them into book form which would be readable, fun and instructive for casual readers, but which would be helpful to other teachers who needed illustrations in their own teaching.

Now, however, my book will need to be therapy for me. My hope is that it will be helpful to others as I recount my own process of mourning, coupled with an increase in faith that God is still at work in my world. Dependence upon His promises during the fourteen months of Howard's illness was a spiritual experience for both of us. It proved to be a time of deep bonding and a poignant valedictory as he quietly and calmly faced an experience I could only share as we waited and prepared for it together.

Chapter 2

~

Change of Plans

W e never expected cancer to hit our family. Surely this was unrealistic and was simply an attitude common to many of us—such things happen to other people, not to us! Howard's mother had died as a result of cancer as had two of her sisters. Of his thirteen siblings, three have already battled cancer and it has also attacked a niece. We were unrealistic when we ignored the family history. But Howard, in his planning and with his methodical, accountant's mindset, had purchased cancer hospital insurance years earlier, even though I viewed it as a waste of money! Once again I was forced to tell him that he had done the right thing. He usually made the right decisions, and I always hated to admit it!

During our fifty-two years together in a strong and mutually satisfying marriage, I was the aggressive, outgoing, up-front partner. Howard was the one behind the scenes, quiet but firm in his support of me. In the days long before it became prudent for men to shed their chauvinism, Howard recognized me as an individual in my own right. He knew that God had given me certain abilities and that he, Howard, had been granted completely different ones. Just as he knew that he must pursue the course for which he was equipped, he understood that I must accomplish my own goals with my own abilities. He was my greatest support. He took pride in my efforts and accomplishments, often embarrassing me by boasting to someone about something I had just done. It never occurred to me that I was limited in any way except by those limitations I imposed upon myself.

When the decades of the '70s and '80s brought women's rights to the forefront of political argument, I already thought of myself as a liberated woman! My husband and children, as well as my parents, always assumed I could do anything I desired, so I usually did just that. The one thing I learned first and quickest after Howard's death was the fact that I was not liberated at all. I had depended upon him more than I ever could have imagined. My life became a series of first-time experiences—alone—and I realized this is something faced by each of us who has had a long relationship with a marriage partner. Divorce surely imposes some of the same emotions. Nor are men immune to the lonely feelings of grief. Death of a child or of close friends or family members must cause the same sense of aloneness. We then are forced to learn how to do, alone, those things we once shared with another. One forceful lesson I learned immediately: never again will I be judgmental of someone who reacts to this personal loss in a manner unlike my own reaction. Grief is a very personal experience, and a lonely one.

Howard and Frances Cooke

Howard in 1993

Chapter 3

Facing Trauma

In 1994, the year of our 50th wedding anniversary, I had suffered a ruptured cerebral aneurysm. It happened in the early morning hours without warning. Howard's immediate reaction in calling the emergency rescue squad afforded me life-saving attention. Even though I recall nothing of the weeks immediately following surgery, I am told of Howard's constant care and attendance at my bedside. Our doctor still today often recalls when I am in his office that every time he saw me in the hospital, Howard was sitting right there with me. The hospital food was in a real slump. (It was terrible!) Howard took to the hospital my silverware because I refused to eat with the provided plastic utensils! He treated me to strawberries—out of season—to entice me to eat. (It didn't work!) He frequently called friends as well as our daughters and other family members to report on my condition.

After I returned home he was nurse, cook, and provider of every attention I could possibly demand. Later, when I realized what had taken place in my life during those weeks of illness and months of recuperation, I wondered why my life had been spared. Doctors had told the family my chances of recovery were limited. It was assumed that, should I recover, there would be some permanent impairment, and the family was warned to expect that. However, I did recover and the lasting effects have been minimal. Why did I not die?

Exactly a year following my illness, Howard was diagnosed with pancreatic cancer. Now it became my turn to care and nurse and love him back to health. Instead, we were both told he had only a very few months left. Now I knew I had been spared for this time. Perhaps God's mission for me now was to be with my husband as he knowingly faced death.

The months ahead were agonizingly heart-breaking. Howard immediately told the doctors he would not undergo chemotherapy treatment, and they concurred because of the location and extensive reach of the tumors. The surgeon bluntly told us to get our affairs in order, and we informed him they were already in order! Twice Howard endured critical surgery to give him relief, but there was no way to remove the cancer which had already invaded stomach, glands, intestines and arteries. We adjusted his diet to make eating more comfortable. He lost weight and strength, but not once—never!—did he complain. He refused to admit to having pain. He just always described it as "discomfort."

The second surgery left him weak and he was never able to walk again. Nine days of physical therapy in a nursing home, undertaken at his request, produced no improvement, and I decided to take him home. From then until his death several months later, I was his nurse. We secured home health care with an attendant coming to the house two or three days each week to care for him a couple of hours while I did errands. Nurses came once a week to change IV equipment and were always on call if I needed assistance or had questions.

The miracle in all this was apparent to both of us. Howard was a very private person, and I would never have imagined that he would allow me to do for him what his illness required. I bathed him, and together we mastered the art of turning from one side to the other. Putting clean linens on his bed was a challenge, but we conquered that, too. I learned to shave him and even learned to trim his mustache to his satisfaction. His barber came frequently to cut his hair, always refusing to accept payment. I mastered the IV which he required around the clock. It was a real accomplishment for me to replace the IV bag and to adjust it when it malfunctioned, for I have absolutely no aptitude for managing equipment or machinery. Neither had I any calling to be a nurse. Even as a child, when other girls played "nurse," I did not dream of becoming one. The last surgery left Howard with a colostomy incision and an ileostomy bag. The latter must be changed as often as every two hours, which I was instructed in how to do. I learned it was quite an art and, surprisingly, I became expert. At the nursing home and on subsequent hospital stays, I found myself teaching aides and even nurses the procedure. At home, I set my alarm clock for every two hours, all night, in order to prevent overflow or leakage of the bag.

We had been warned that two or three months were all we could expect to have together after the diagnosis was made. Howard lived fourteen months! And they were good! I had, at first, known real panic when I realized his death coming so soon would quickly reduce my income drastically. We now had accumulating medical bills, and there were other expenses which I would be unable to meet. With the help of Anita, the daughter with a business aptitude, together we were able to talk about financial plans.

We never had to say to each other that he was dying. That was understood. We shared that awareness through our planning for my future, rather than by talking "death." As a result, while I am far from having the freedom of spending as I did while Howard lived and received an income, I have been able to maintain a lifestyle somewhat similar to the one we enjoyed together.

Our older daughter, Marilyn, also contributed greatly to our security during those months. Seven months before her father's death she graduated from nursing school and he was able to celebrate the event with her by attending the graduation and pinning ceremony. We had always known that nursing was her calling. Her choice of college after high school was nursing school, but she failed to complete the training. Now, at age 48, she had completed school, and the dreams of her parents—especially her father—were realized. During the remainder of Howard's illness, Marilyn was a constant support and unfailing help. Doctors talked freely to her, explaining procedures and the progression of her Dad's illness. She, in turn, was then able to translate the medical language for me and, when decisions needed to be made, it was her rapport with the doctors and her father's confidence in her which gave us direction.

Perhaps the greatest miracle that occurred during those months of illness was the strengthening of personal faith, the absolute assurance of God's presence with us. The deepening of our emotional relationship with each other happened as a result of this shared spiritual experience. Today friends comment to me that I had a really hard time during Howard's illness. Amazingly, I don't recall it that way. Yes, there was great anxiety. There were moments when I was heartsick and frightened. There were times when I was so tired I felt I could not continue. Occasionally Howard and I even snapped at each other; he was tired, too. There were times when I suffered for him, fervently wishing I could spare him this illness. But in those darkest of moments—and there were lots of them—there was the unspoken awareness deep within me that this could not be all there is to our existence. I could literally feel God's presence as a blanket enfolding us. Prior to this experience I had always known that God makes and keeps the promise that He is always with us. I knew all the right phrases, all the words to say which would describe His presence. Now I don't need to struggle for pretty words; I have felt deeply God's presence with me when I desperately needed Him. And it was comforting!

There were, however, moments of unbearable hurting when I berated God for the pain we suffered. He already knew what was in my heart, so I vocally questioned why He couldn't come up with a better plan for the way our lives should end. A better plan, such as letting partners go together! A friend admonished me to not ask God, "Why?," to never question Him. Oh, but I do! I talk to Him constantly. When I question God, I truly want an answer, and when I wait for it I always receive the answer. That is how I grow and mature in faith, which always seems to happen in times of heartache and suffering. It never becomes a weaker faith. Someone has called the broken heart "an entranceway for God." Our grieving was truly an encounter with the Eternal.

There was much I learned about my husband, also, much I had appreciated in an off-hand way but which now gave me real joy and insight into his true nature. He was a man of faith—quiet, unquestioning faith. He was the most patient human being I have ever known, a trait for which I continue to struggle. To endure the indignity of the illness which beset him, without complaint, was an astounding example of patience and even temper. To accept my inept nursing ministrations, also without complaint and always with expressed gratitude, revealed an even greater degree of patience. Since his death I recall that time in our lives as not only revealing, but as a source of encouragement for me. He continues to inspire and support me by the memory of his fortitude and sweet patience.

A cliché repeated to me by well-meaning but inexperienced friends was, "The first year will be the hardest." Then they would remind me that after the first year I would simply be repeating events and days which I had by now already experienced once alone, and thus would not suffer so much pain again. I can only say they haven't been there! Each day continues to bring a first-time experience. There is often a new emotion, a new scene, a memory, a thought. Life is filled with daily first-time experiences. These episodes, which occur for the first time for the one left behind and which must now be faced alone by that partner, are the focus of my thoughts as I write. They do not occur in lockstep fashion, one after the other, some repeating themselves endlessly. They are recorded here by type of experience, not in any chronological order. They did not happen to me in consecutive, marching order. I have discovered there is new, revealing meaning in the phrase, "Today is the first day of the rest of your life." As the days pass endlessly, I am convinced there will never be a time when I am healed of all hurt and grief. Years cannot erase the lifetime shared with my mainstay, the anchor whom I called husband.

Chapter 4

Attacking the Plumbing

To prepare oneself for the death of a loved one is, perhaps, necessary, but it is nearly impossible. No matter how much thought has been given to the time when they are no longer with you, there are always surprises. A friend and I laugh that a light bulb has become the symbol of our aloneness! How surprised I was when the bulb in my reading lamp needed to be replaced. Always, when that had been necessary, it was my habit to fume and then caustically say, "Howard, this bulb has burned out again!" And Howard, in his own good time, would dutifully replace the bulb.

Now I found myself having to check the supply of bulbs, look in all the lamps and fixtures to determine what size he had used in each, and then to cry while I screwed in the needed replacement. The job became even more tedious and difficult when bulbs in the microwave, the oven, ceiling lights, outdoor lights, and especially tubes in the bathroom and kitchen fixtures burned out. I had never given a single thought to their mechanisms. Climbing the ladder to replace overhead bulbs was dangerous, but I just dared the ladder to tip me off! I was angrily determined to solve all the problems by myself, and to have a good cry while doing so. My friend, who has been widowed more than twenty years, now moves around with a walker and can be excused for her inability to replace light bulbs. I can't so easily forgive myself. Instead there is the feeling of guilt and helplessness. I had assumed without question that my husband would always handle such mundane chores without need for me to bother my pretty head with those petty tasks. Now they don't seem so petty.

The practical chores I had to assume increased as the days dragged by. Plumbing was a deep dark mystery to me. During the months of illness, Howard had helped me compile a list of the service providers he used, with telephone numbers, so I did know who our regular plumber was. But you can't call a plumber every time a faucet drips, or a toilet runs continuously after being flushed. Fortunately for me, Howard had an obsession with books—the ownership of books. He did not wish to check them out at the library; he wanted to have them on his own shelves.

Now I was regretting every complaint I had uttered about the money he "wasted" on books. There, on the shelves, I found help! There were fix-it-yourself manuals of every description, books of skills and tools, do-it-yourself projects, helpful hints for the family handyman, and one book which became my treasure trove: *How to Fix Damn Near Everything*. I read and I researched and when there were plumbing problems, I approached them with book in hand. First problems were in the bathroom. When flushed, the toilet tank refused to fill properly and the water ran on and on. To the books I went! The drawings helped me locate the source of the problem and gave instructions on removal of the offending parts. It was simple to make note of what the replacement parts were called, and to make diagrams, before going to the hardware store. By doing so I never felt quite so stupid when talking to a salesman or clerk. Usually that was not necessary, for often I located what I thought was needed. Back home again diagrams and pictures in the books were followed, and I was extremely proud of myself when the problem had been successfully corrected. But there was still one problem—there was no one to whom to brag!

When the bathrooms at the beach house also gave trouble, even without benefit of the books, I was able to spot the problems. New difficulties arose, however, at the hardware store. There were so many kinds of replacement parts, how could one determine which is the correct one to buy? Again, an easy solution: since they were inexpensive, buy two different ones. Surely one would work! It did, and my successful record was unbroken.

It quickly became necessary to assume total responsibility for other household needs which traditionally had belonged to the man of the family. Couples joke that taking out the trash and emptying waste baskets are the husband's duty. It was surely no joking matter to me now. First it was necessary to become familiar with the scheduled trash days—one for household garbage, another day for yard waste, and still another day for recyclables. Containers for each type of trash were specified by the city waste removal department. I found myself grumbling and crying every day when struggling with the minute details and requirements. Again I felt guilt; I had taken so much for granted.

The dangerous job of cleaning the gutters was not made easier when I faced the truth— there would be no gutters to clean if I had not insisted. Howard had removed the gutters soon after the house was built, and through the years I nagged him to replace them. The house would look more "finished," I argued. Finally he complied with my desires, and now I was reaping the consequences. Refusing to locate a handyman, and determined to do everything myself, one sunny day I placed the ladder against the side of the house and climbed to the gutters. As a nod to caution, I did place a portable telephone on the ground near the ladder, just in case of falling and needing to call for help. Reaching into the gutters, I was having success in pulling out pine straw and debris, when a neighbor spotted me and began berating me loudly enough for the whole neighborhood to hear. With offers to help me with jobs such as that one, she convinced me to come down from the ladder. One later time, I was able to clean the gutters without an audience— all the neighbors were away from their homes. Afterwards, though, I realized I was really tempting fate, so that job has been farmed out to the yard man since that time.

Soon there were much larger projects which I now had to deal with alone. How to talk to workmen about them became a challenge. I wanted to seem knowledgeable and I didn't wish to be overcharged for the work. The latter became a definite concern. A woman alone feels so vulnerable, and there are numerous stories to corroborate her fears. Again, reading as much as possible about the needed repairs, and then very cautiously inquiring of family and friends the range of expected costs, served as a guide. But I continued to make some wrong decisions, which depressed me. Then I remembered that when Howard and I were making decisions together, they were not always the perfect ones. Thus I learned to be as cautious, as prepared, as knowledgeable as possible, and then to accept the outcome.

We had lived in our house for nearly forty years. After we retired, we spent some time and money upgrading and making additions. Roof repairs and new shingles were first. New windows were installed and outdoor siding was replaced. In the kitchen we added cabinets and a new sink. The replacement of lighting fixtures in kitchen and bath was planned, with some fixtures chosen and purchased, but illness put that project on hold. An automatic sump pump needed to be installed to control water flowing under the house. Cracks in the ceilings had occurred at seam lines and Howard had talked with workmen, scheduling some of the work before his illness. All came to a halt. After his death, the daunting task of carrying on our planned work and repairs was still there. It became for me a matter of locating workmen, but the greatest problem was to locate money for the jobs! Then began a juggling exercise. Slowly some of the work was completed, but I continue to be very anxious when the supply of cash is exceeded by the amount needed. Accepting the limitations caused by a reduced income was a real concern. The "alone" partner must still meet all normal costs of home and upkeep, and do so with only one income.

One of the largest projects to undertake was painting the house inside, and my financial situation told me I must do the work myself. Probably an even larger factor in that decision was the determination to do everything my way, by myself. Informed preparation was imperative. In the storeroom were painting supplies from previous jobs, and I determined which could now be used and what additional purchases must be made. A lesson learned many years earlier was helpful now: read all instructions and follow them, no shortcuts! Doing it right saves time and money. When friends and family learned I was painting ceilings, there was an outcry. Of course it was risky and dangerous. Again, I took every precaution possible, but continued to do the work myself. The twin grandchildren, Angela and David, now in their teens, eagerly offered to help, and the three of us wielded paint brushes for days and days during that summer. It was a satisfying accomplishment when a room would be completed, and the rapport with grandchildren was extremely rewarding. We were so proud of our work. Once again the completed paint job was verification of my ability to do the necessary work and chores if only I planned carefully, and if I could just learn to accept graciously the help offered by my willing family.

While working for the Baptist Foundation I had been assigned a company car which I drove all over North Carolina, alone, for speaking engagements, workshops, and visits with donors. I considered myself a safe driver, though my husband accused me of driving too fast. (True!) That was almost the extent of my knowledge about cars. Oil changes, tire rotations, inspections, and practically every required service except pumping gas was taken care of by the office. At home, of course, friend husband was the designated caretaker of the autos. Not any more! Suddenly it became important for me to become familiar with what was under the hood! During his months of illness, Howard had been able to accompany me once for an oil change. He also showed me where he kept all the records of every service performed at the garage. After we knew he would not be able to drive again, he directed and guided me in the sale of one vehicle. After his death, it was easier to drive up to the service departments and explain the work I wanted done. How grateful I was for those months during which he was able to instruct me, but how strong was the guilt that I had waited so long to learn the simple, basic things about the autos I drove. The greatest concern now, after months of coping with the automobile alone, is that I still don't know enough. I must trust the honesty of the mechanics and service departments of the garages which I frequent. If my education were more complete, perhaps there would be less reason to be skeptical about the charges presented after the car has been serviced. I might even have a comeback for those few persons who patronize me with condescending explanations of my problem. One knowledgeable comment by me about the engine noise I was hearing would quickly put an end to the abhorrent practice of condescension. Maybe a suggestion that the mechanic "check the ignition timing advance controls and the EGR valve" would indicate I knew what I was talking about, even though I am female! (Truthfully, I don't know what timing controls and EGR valves are!)

Despite pride in my safe driving record, a collision finally put an end to my boasting. Happily it was not my fault, but the resulting decisions and requirements for reporting, collecting insurance, scheduling repairs, etc. were the same as if I had been responsible for the accident. This was all new for me. I recalled cautions I had read, instructions from drivers' manuals, and what Howard had done on a similar occasion for him. I tried to remain calm—no one was injured—and gracious. Fortunately, it all worked together as it should and the test was weathered. Must the accident be reported to my insurance company if I was not at fault? Does one accept a check from an insurance company before all the work and costs are agreed upon? If so, do you cash it? From which insurance company, yours or the guilty driver's? Must there be more than one quote for cost of repairs? To whom does one go for repairs - dealer, garage, or body shop? Where must I take the car for insurance adjusters? All these things, and many more, were foreign territory for me. My pride kicked in when I realized I had accomplished one more thing, without help or guidance from anyone, for the first time.

Christmas promised to be difficult. Not only was this first one to cause its profound emotional reaction, but simply the work required to continue the family traditions seemed astronomical. The tree must be a live one and it must be seven feet tall! Those were the requirements we had always met, and I was determined to do so this year.

Howard and I had always chosen the tree together. In earlier years we, with the children, had cut our tree from Dad Lewis's farm in a tradition that involved the entire Lewis family. When that ceased to be available to us, we had most often bought our tree from a lot at Farmers' Market. Since that was familiar to me, I chose to go there on a week day when the crowd would be small. Selecting the right tree was no problem because Howard had always accepted my decision on that. The salesman was exceedingly helpful and understanding when my problem with removing the tree from the trunk of the car was explained, and he wrapped and tied it so that job would be easier.

At home I struggled to lift, pull, tug and finally drag the tree to a tub of water where it would stand until I wished to take it inside. First, the ornaments and decorations had to be gathered which required a climb on a ladder to the top shelves in an outside storage room. Carefully lodging the ladder, I was able to retrieve the boxes, one at a time, exercising extreme caution as I climbed up and down. The tree holder which we had been using for several years proved to have been a perfect investment for me now. It had a pin standing upright in the middle and the tree had a hole bored in the trunk which fit onto the pin. Once inside the house with the tree, I could leverage it onto the pin in the stand, and voilà, there was my tree, upright and straight. It was difficult to wait until I could tell the family how smart I was to do it all by myself!

The next chore was stringing the lights. Howard had always—always!—done that job. It was tedious and I disliked the boredom of the hours necessary to get hundreds of lights on just the right limbs. I protested to the empty air, cried, fussed and cried some more, but the job was finally accomplished. Placing the ornaments had also been a shared job but I managed to get everything in its customary place. The family stockings were all hung on the mantle, the tables held their customary Christmas arrangements, and I was almost belligerent in my pride. "See," I wanted to say, "I can do it myself and I will do it!"

Those protestations of "doing it myself" give a picture of me as stubborn and difficult to get along with. Truly, I did not wish to appear that way. My world was no longer normal. How could parental, adult control of life be maintained if my children's lives were also in turmoil by having to assist me with every problem I encountered? There was no need to become a cantankerous despot. Rather, I made a firm resolve to face the new challenges of life with grace and humor—if possible! But to myself, in my aloneness, I wallowed in screams and sobs and protested every change in my life which I had neither ordered nor invited.

After his retirement, our third bedroom was converted into a combination guest room and office for Howard. There he spent hours at his desk, and I had impatiently wondered, sometimes aloud to him, what he could find to do all those hours. Now I soon discovered! Bills to be paid never seemed to be accurate or understandable. Many required clarification and the necessary telephone calls were seldom answered by a human being but by a machine. That, of course, resulted in hours of waiting for return calls before the matter was resolved. Frustration and anger mounted in intensity. Insurances had to be monitored, magazines and books had to be cancelled, records changed from our name to my name. Often a death certificate was required which resulted in days of waiting for responses. Nothing was accomplished with a single effort. Everything took multiple days and efforts to complete. Every project seemed to demand numerous conversations and correspondence. I had discovered what Howard did all day at his desk, and now all the problems were mine to solve—alone!

Chapter 5

Emotional Blockade

E motional "firsts," just as practical ones, can overwhelm, even those experiences which may seem insignificant. Mail addressed to "the single person at this address" began immediately to fill my mailbox and I was appalled. Telephone calls for "Mr." Cooke were—and still remain—a constant source of hurt, despair and anger. The letters were easily disposed of; I just threw them away unopened and in time they stopped coming with any frequency. The telephone continues to be another matter. An answering machine controls some of the phone traffic. However, when I do answer the phone and the caller asks to speak to Mr. Cooke, I just quietly hang up.

Good manners are not required. I did not invite the caller into my home just as I would not invite inside any other total stranger who appeared at my door. It is a simple safety issue. There is no reason for me to offer any explanation and I never, never tell a caller my husband is deceased or that I live alone. The safest and easiest way to take care of unwelcome callers, apart from not answering the phone, is the simple act of hanging up. The emotional damage, however, continues to take its toll as each call reminds me graphically how changed my life has become. (Note: there are devices and programs provided by the phone companies which may be installed to solve this problem—if you can afford the monthly fee! And now there is the "Do Not Call" program which helps somewhat.)

Mail addressed to Mr. and Mrs. is an entirely different matter. Vendors with whom we dealt on a regular basis were advised of Howard's death, as were personal friends in those companies. After my official correspondence resulted in no change of the way the mail was addressed, I wrote personal letters to individuals we knew in those offices. I politely acknowledged my understanding of the problems they faced in getting company addresses quickly corrected, but expressed my hope they could soon do so. Since, in each case, they had known my husband and had been personally advised of his death, I would include a plaint about my pain in receiving jointly addressed mail. When "we" continue even now to receive holiday greetings and personal messages, I know they are generated *en masse* by office personnel and are not even remotely personal in nature. The one whose signature is on it has neither seen nor signed the letter. Neither has he acknowledged nor followed through on my personal request of him. In effect, my husband and I were nothing more than names used in promotion of a product or service. My reaction now is to feel no guilt as I drop their names and their businesses from my list of friends and contacts. Their public relations mailings fail completely with me!

In the week following Howard's death, Anita, her husband, Steve, and their family were with me before returning to their home in Pennsylvania. They were a profound comfort. My concern was for them, especially for the young children, some of whom had been at the bedside when their grandfather died. During those days there were innumerable tasks to be completed which kept us involved and perhaps helped to lessen the pain which would come with too much time to think. Even while busy with essentials, I felt as though I moved in a suffocating fog which would never lift.

Steve was the cook of his family and in prior, happier days had treated us to bountiful breakfasts, especially when we were at the beach together. On that first Sunday morning he offered to prepare breakfast. The table was opened to accommodate all the family, places were laid and we looked forward to a sit-down meal together, the first in days. When we took our places at the table, I beamed on my family, and then was overcome with grief. This was the first time of hosting a family meal without my partner. There was a great empty place at the table, one never to be filled again. I was truly, utterly immersed in the reality that I was alone. My anguish and heartache could not be contained. No experience has been so vivid, so terribly indicative of what lay ahead for me. I tried to hide my tears but they were like a swollen river rushing over a dam. This was a first-time emotional experience which would be repeated, time and again, in the days and years ahead.

While it is true that observing special days and anniversaries can be particularly difficult early in one's grieving, the anguish and tears can be just as intense in later years. I have recently observed a wedding anniversary, not the first since Howard's death but the most emotionally poignant. Even our 52nd, just two months after he died, did not cause this crushing despair, the sense of utter defeat and sadness. The feeling that I had been abandoned would not leave me and it was nearly impossible to rouse myself to the routine tasks of the day. Why should this year have been different?

There is no particular significance to a 56th anniversary. There had been no warnings, no emotional crises to prepare me for the intense dejection I felt when I awoke. Now I wondered how I would get through the day. Before this, I had been busily painting my house for several weeks, a job not yet completed. A Sunday School lesson needed to be studied and prepared for presentation. Grandchildren, out of school, should be invited to spend part of the day with me. Still, it seemed too much to ask that I generate enough energy or interest to do anything. The paralysis of grief had me tied, inert.

Howard's grave has never been without flowers. Each change of season, and at other special times of the year, the container on his gravestone is replenished with fresh arrangements. (Years before this, when my work involved estate planning conferences, I always encouraged the participants to establish charitable memorial funds in the names of their loved ones. Thus, on significant days afterward, they could make a gift to the memorial fund. They would be continuing the influence and the name of the deceased person, permanently. There would be no need to purchase artificial flowers to fade, deteriorate, and perhaps be stolen from the grave. Now I do both—I make a gift to Howard's memorial fund, and I also have a compulsion to put flowers on the grave. That is a tangible gift. It makes *me* feel better. So much for having all the answers before you've met the problem!)

It was now time, on this 56th anniversary, to place fall flowers on the grave and I was determined to spend the entire day, if necessary, on that project. The urn must first be retrieved from the cemetery, ten miles away. A trip to the flower shop was required to buy flowers of just the right color. Hours were needed to arrange them artistically and firmly in the vase, as though Howard would personally approve or disapprove. Finally another trip must be made to the cemetery to place the new arrangement on the grave. It took me all day. I cried some, but I was busy. Howard and I carried on imaginary conversations, most of them about the inability of those blasted flowers to stay in the precise position where I placed them in the container! When the job was finished, I felt complete. The day had not been a total loss, for something practical had been accomplished. Then I headed to my mother's home to finish my crying.

Mother was widowed just four years before I was. She had experienced all that I now began to experience. Her compassion and understanding, her wisdom and example, her knowledge of just the right things to say have made her my confidante, my encourager, my therapist, my friend. So, at the end of that day I cried with her, we recalled the good times, we laughed at some memories, and I went home un-burdened.

Having someone in your life with whom you can freely share your deepest feelings is an immense blessing. No person, however, not even the spouse for whom you mourn, could always be attuned to your emotional needs. (You often fail them, too!) There will still be disappointments and times when you feel no one understands, no one cares.

This recent anniversary helped me examine the exaggerated expectations I have of family and friends, and of the feelings they must have as they try to relate to me and my grieving. Mother always writes a letter, an anniversary message, in which she tells me how deeply Howard was loved as a "son," and she always apologizes for the objections she and Dad expressed when I married at such a young age, so many years ago. My sisters are faithful in telephoning or writing to tell me they are thinking of me on that day. One friend, who was often the object of Howard's teasing, always writes and recalls the fun times with "What's-his-name," a moniker he overheard her apply to him once when she couldn't immediately recall his name!

It was the reaction of my daughters that caused me to make a more critical appraisal of and attention to their own grief. I was not the only person remembering and suffering a loss on the anniversary day. Both girls had unique personal relationships with their Dad. They knew he had such pride in their character, their intelligence, their achievements and their beauty. Neither ever doubted his love was deep and sincere. Both girls talked with me by telephone on that anniversary, but neither mentioned her father nor the occasion. I had no doubt they were aware of the date for we had had conversations earlier in the week. I was somewhat puzzled. Had they simply forgotten because of their own busy lives? I felt guilty because I was hurt. I was sure, in my heart, they cared and simply chose to remain silent, possibly because it hurt them too much to speak of it. In a later conversation about my feelings, one daughter said, "But Mom, I didn't know what to say to you!"

That opened my eyes. Of course you can't wish someone like me a happy anniversary. What do you say on such an occasion? I recalled an experience exactly a month after Howard's death. It was Mother's 91st birthday. Our large family always gathered in celebration of our parents' birthdays. I expected this one to be no different and had been told we would celebrate with cake and ice cream in the evening. It would be difficult for me, but I was sure I had the courage to endure it. After all, it was for my mother. The yard at the farmhouse, when I arrived, was filled with cars with barely room to park. The planned small family gathering for dessert seemed to have grown larger. The house was crowded, and the dining table was filled with covered dishes of food. This was a big departure from the cake and ice cream I expected. My offering was a freezer of ice cream, certainly not a casserole! I was stunned but tried to conceal it. Siblings, their spouses and children, dozens of grandchildren were laughing, talking and enjoying the party, which was natural. Until I entered the room! I was like a stranger intruding on their fun and no one could manage to utter more than a weak "hi" to me. I'm the oldest child in the family and am *always* in attendance at every family occasion, but I had never felt so invisible. No one knew what to say to me! I was devastated. I fled to my car.

Now, four years later, my own daughter says, "I didn't know what to say to you!" That's it! Few of us know how to face the grief of someone else. Most of us are tongue-tied; we just keep silent and ignore the whole subject, heaping more desolation on the one who is already suffering beyond description. Taking a lesson from my mother and my sisters, I explained to my daughter that all she needs to say is, "Mom, I know what today is", or, "I am thinking of you in a special way today." In addition, I wanted someone to *say* Howard's name, as though he were still a presence with us. For he is!

I am a couple, still. Singular—a couple! There are many Scripture passages on the relationship of husband and wife, and one is vividly meaningful to me. In Ephesians, Paul quotes the passage from Genesis which states, in part, "...a man will leave his father and mother and unite with his wife and the two will become one." In the days immediately following Howard's death, I experienced the sensation of having been severed in half. I would rise from my chair and literally wait for the other half of my body to be rejoined to me. It was strangely both a physical and an emotional severance. Explain it, I can't. But to me it was a definite need to wait for my body to be made whole again before I could take a step. Today, I still feel complete only as Howard's wife. I am a couple! My wedding rings are still on my left hand. Many of Howard's best jackets and business suits still hang in our closet. Even his pipes still rest in their ashtrays. Most of his clothing was long ago given to charity, but I find it difficult to dismiss him altogether from the house. To some, this may be an unhealthy attitude. But for me it continues to provide a sense of his presence. It keeps me in touch with him. Recently I have been able to recognize and to say that I am now Howard's widow, no longer a wife. Yet I feel that will never be completely true. I utterly detest the word "widow." To me it is the ugliest word in the English language, and I am unwilling to hear it applied to me.

When I did dispose of clothing, it was done by degrees. It was never difficult to pack up for charity the warm-up suits and casual clothing Howard had worn during the months of illness when he was housebound. Underwear, socks, ties, etc. were simply trashed. Next to go to charity were the beach clothes, all the shorts and very casual things he had worn there. Still left in the closets were the business suits and sports jackets which he had worn daily to work. They were so personal—so "Howard"—I reluctantly considered where they could be directed to do the most good. At Christmas, when a local mission gave gifts to homeless persons at a real party, the packages all tied up as Christmas gifts, I was able to part with some of the clothes because I knew they would truly help a less fortunate person. When I took them to the mission, however, I made sure the director knew of my sacrifice! Later I called the same mission to pick up some remaining clothes. The suits were cleaned and on hangers when the driver came to the door. Giving them to him, I wept and told him to "take care of these things" because they had been my husband's. The poor man looked at me as though I were out of my mind, and justly so, for I even embarrassed myself. Other items of clothing I cannot part with—the Stetson hat he bought on a trip to the West, the cowboy boots he bought for himself in Cody, Wyoming, a cap from Pebble Beach, California, a plaid tam from Scotland. Each holds dear memories for me, and I keep them because it hurts to think of giving his treasures away.

Tears flow so easily and so unexpectedly, a response that continues to surprise me. Emotions lie just at the surface. After spending a few days at the beach with my children, I needed to return to Raleigh for an early morning appointment. I slipped out of the house before the family awoke and without having had breakfast. Within an hour hunger led me to stop at a fast food restaurant. After receiving my order, I found a table by the window and knew there was time enough to enjoy a quick bite. Then, before I could sweeten the coffee, tears nearly choked me as they flowed without warning. This was a stop Howard and I had frequently made on our trips to and from the beach and to stop there was natural for me. It was almost impossible to believe that a fast food chain was making me cry!

Valentine's Day was not an important observance for us. We more often gave gifts to our daughters and, when they were young, always helped them write Valentine messages to all their friends. On the first February 14th after

Howard's death, I was at the Baptist Building doing my daily volunteer work for Woman's Missionary Union. My former co-workers at The Baptist Foundation, anxious about my emotional state on this sentimental day, came to my work place with a large bouquet of flowers. Of course the tears flowed, but I was deeply touched by their caring and remembering. That Valentine's Day, and every subsequent day, I have been forced to acknowledge to myself that I am no longer "first" on anyone's love list! My children love me, but they have mates of their own. My mother loves me, but she has nine other children to love equally. God loves me, but not above all others! Only Howard put me first in his heart, and that I no longer have.

One day I laughed! I was stunned. Did that bubble which rose in my throat really expel itself as a chuckle? My next emotion was one of guilt. How could I find anything about which to laugh? I am not supposed to laugh; I am a widow! And then there followed a great sense of relief. Here I was, watching a silly TV program, and it actually was funny. The heartache which had gripped me eased just a little. I began to feel more like a normal human being, not like one in a stupor.

Not long afterwards the family and I could recall humorous times we had shared. We laughed at habits and mannerisms of their father about which we had always laughed and teased him: how he'd shake his finger in a "no, no;" how he'd stir his coffee and stir—and stir—and stir until I'd remind him it was all well mixed now and he was making a hole in the cup; how he'd insist on clearing the table after a meal and then would rinse the dishes so well there was little need to wash them; how he'd put his pipe in his mouth and then contentedly ride the lawnmower for hours! We would nearly double over in stitches when we remembered his tendency to never answer a question until he'd had sufficient time to think it through thoroughly, often hours later! Particularly recalled was the day I had asked him, early in the morning, what was the product produced by the company which we were driving past. Silence! Ten hours later, as we returned from our trip and again passed the building, he said, as though no time had elapsed, "I don't know, but I think ...." Oh, it was good to laugh again. It was the beginning of life returning to some sense of normalcy. Yet we still missed that one important person.

Friends and family, who truly wish to be helpful, sometimes remind me of the wonderful memories I have of the exciting trips we took, events we enjoyed together, music for which we had the same preference, and the years of togetherness shared with my best friend, my husband, my soul mate. I concur, and then in a lighter mood I reply, "But memories don't keep my feet warm at night in bed!"

Emotions, always fragile, are more so now.

Howard's grave with flowers
Cemetery in Knightdale, North Carolina

Chapter 6

Obstructions—Spiritual Life and Worship

Returning to church worship services was one of the most difficult acts but one which I needed and desired. The funeral service had been held in the church sanctuary at the request of our daughters. It had been planned by Howard and me that, when the time came, we would take advantage of the convenience of the funeral home chapel. Anita particularly objected, wishing to surround herself and her children with the worshipful atmosphere of the church where we had always worshipped, where her parents had held places of leadership, and where she had been taught spiritual values. I finally agreed and steeled myself for my eventual return to worship services. I anticipated no problem since I was making a conscious decision to hold the service in the sanctuary. It would therefore be possible to anticipate and to plan to control my emotional reaction when I should return to church.

As part of the funeral service, I had requested that the congregation join the family in singing the familiar doxology, "Praise God From Whom All Blessings Flow." There should be no problem when that would frequently be sung at future worship services, since I could prepare my heart for that eventuality, also. That proved to be the case. But other events at church worship services took me by complete surprise and on my first Sunday returning I rushed away after the services without being able to speak to anyone.

Howard had been a faithful deacon and had always taken his turn in the ritual of receiving the offering. It was the group of deacons, filing down the aisles to receive the plates at the altar, which brought me painful and unexpected anguish. Someone was missing! Never to be in his regular place again! I was devastated and fought to maintain some semblance of composure for the remainder of the service.

Like most persons who are regular in attendance, Howard and I had a favorite pew, one which we laughingly said we had carved with our names. I have never been able to sit there again. I moved to another part of the sanctuary, a place where he would have never wished to sit.

Within a few months after his death, our 125-year-old church voted to relocate to another part of the city. I was opposed and voted my conviction, even though I knew the decision was assuredly a vote for relocation. Needless to say, when the tally was announced I was not surprised but I was tearful. However, I surprised even myself by feeling that it had been a deliberate vote to hurt me! I had just lost my husband and now the congregation was taking another cherished thing away from me! Even today, months later, I am astonished that I could put such a meaning to the church's action. In another time I would have had no patience with anyone whose thoughts were so illogical. Having always prided myself on clear thinking, this was an unwelcome and senseless feeling. Bouncing around in my brain was the truth that the people had no such thoughts, but I needed more misery in which to wallow!

Our church ordains newly elected deacons in an annual service at the beginning of each year. At a recent ordination service I was again brought to tears by memories. Several years after Howard began his service as a deacon, I was given the opportunity to also serve on the deacon body. Two other women of our membership had been elected in years prior to this, but I was the first woman to serve at the same time as her husband. We joked that, at deacons' meetings, we would not sit together so we could not be accused of "bloc" voting. My ordination was a stirring experience for me, and Howard participated in the "laying on of hands," which is the defining point of the service. The experience was made more meaningful for me because of my husband's affirmation as he joined others in accepting me for this ministry.

Recently the church elected to the diaconate two women whose husbands also serve as deacons. One of those men is suffering from cancer but was able to participate in the ordination. When I watched him lay hands on his wife's head in an act of ordaining her for this special ministry, I could not contain the tears. His illness is considered terminal but his wife, like I, will always have the precious memory of a loved husband participating in one of the most meaningful acts of her Christian experience. I had not prepared myself for the way I felt at that service, and again I was surprised by my tearful reaction.

There are times when I withdraw from worship, when I focus on something outside the service which is not part of the order of worship. A hymn which was Howard's favorite, a sermon text or Scripture which reminds me of so many moments shared with him, or music which is powerful and moving will cause me to declare to myself, "I'm not here—

get thee out of this place—direct your thoughts elsewhere!" There are other times, however, when those very same instances move me to gratitude and worship of the One who gave me life and husband and children and family and.... Why do I react so differently to familiar experiences? That is another of the unexplainable and surprising emotions of this loss and grief I endure. I never know when or why I will be suddenly overcome by grief, or by joy!

My understanding of God's promises of life eternal is clearer today. The hope it gives to believers is a sustaining miracle. I would be destroyed without it. A cartoon in "The Family Circus" recently illustrated, so vividly, the comfort afforded by this promise. One lady, meeting another on the street, stopped her to express her sympathy. "I am so sorry," she said, "to hear that you have lost your husband." To which the newly widowed one replied, "Oh, I haven't lost him. I know exactly where he is!" No one remains entirely devastated when they have that hope and assurance from God!

My Sunday School class is composed of women in my age bracket, "Senior Adults" they call us. Most are widowed. In prior years, as I taught them on Sundays, I commended them for their strength and their faithfulness. They seemed to deal with life alone with great purpose, and I often told them if I should be widowed as they, my prayer was that I should have the same strength which they possessed. My prayer was answered—I do! Faith in God's promises has sustained me. That, however, does not mean there are no tears, no hurt. Believers are neither promised nor given a carefree, painless existence. God's promise to us is that He will be with us through every sorrow and hurt—and He is. That is the miracle of His presence in our lives. Today when I teach a Bible lesson, I speak with the assurance of one who has been *through* shadows and is not lost in them.

Chapter 7

Inertia Overcome

The days following the funeral service were a blur. So much to do, and I unable to concentrate. My whole body seemed traumatized, and perhaps it was. Carrying out the legal requirements was imperative and somehow I managed. The clerk of court was compassionate and *helpful* in the probate process. Each visit to that office resulted in one more thing accomplished, and one thing at a time seemed to be all of which I was capable. Back home, I just sat. I, who had always attacked several tasks simultaneously, with a work ethic that did not allow for a single wasted minute, lacked the will to even pick up a magazine or book to read. I was a zombie! Sleep was non-existent; meals were prepared and eaten as though I were in a stupor. Underlying those early, agonizingly painful days, were two constant thoughts: I am alone—but God is with me. The first devastated me and the second kept me going. The great surprise to me was, that even though Howard's death had been expected and preparations made, nothing could have prepared me for the desolate feeling of aloneness.

There was a difference between loneliness and being alone. I was not afraid to be alone in my house. There were none of the nighttime fears I had heard others express, partially because they had already been experienced during the hospitalization days. When I began to return to normal activities, there was never time to feel lonely as I stayed busy with numerous activities. Even as new challenges commanded my attention, I did not suffer the loneliness which is characterized by feelings of withdrawal, abandonment and complete helplessness. Contrarily, I was determined to meet the daily needs, but I always knew I must do so alone. In my mind, there was a great difference between the despair of loneliness and the awareness of being alone as I coped with new circumstances.

The beach condo, our personal retreat place, was now out of the picture for me. Never could I go back to it! Then, however, I was advised that the probate papers filed in our home county must be taken to Brunswick County (the location of the beach property) and recorded there also. I had no choice. The three-hour drive was spent imagining each step of arrival and preparing my emotional state for the time I would be at the condo—my first time there without my husband. I am not even sure I uttered a prayer about it. So convinced was I that it could never again serve any good purpose for me, I had in conversation with Howard told him my feelings and had secured his permission to sell the condo.

What a wonderful surprise to discover on arrival that I was home! Secure, safe, it had now become my retreat, not "ours." When I walked to the beach and stood watching the waves roll in nonstop, it was then that I was able to voice my prayer of thanksgiving. Today, it is still my retreat. Each time I cross the dunes and see before me His magnificent ocean, it is then I thank God for creating such powerful beauty and I always tearfully thank Howard for providing it for me. The contemplation of such extraordinary beauty has been rightly described, for me, as "a healing response for a crushed soul."

> Today I walked beside the sea,
> The stormy sea,
> The roiling sea,
> And there was God revealed to me.
> This morn I walked beside the sea,
> The quiet sea,
> The sparkling sea,
> And in the calm God spoke to me.
> Whene'er I walk beside the sea,
> A morning sea,
> Or evening sea,
> God's always there assuring me.
> Whene'er I leave the mighty sea,
> My soul restored,
> My life becalmed,
> I thank God who provides it for me.
>
> *flc*

When I take my daily walks on the shore, God and I often carry on long conversations. I tell Him that life is not complete without my soul mate; that I feel deprived; that Howard and I had anticipated walking this beach together into our *real* old age. After that is said, then I can thank Him for the beauty and the magic of the ocean and for the time He allows me to enjoy it. In turn I am reminded that He is, indeed, the Creator of all the earth and that He cares about my pain and grief. My thoughts inevitably turn to gratitude for my life with Howard and for the provisions of life which God enabled him to supply for us, including the beach retreat. I repeat to myself a rhyme which is framed and hangs on the wall in the condo. It was given to us by our daughter, Marilyn, and at our 50th anniversary I repeated it in a toast to him in gratitude for his provision for us as husband and father. He had faithfully given us the necessities of life, filled our house with books for enjoyment and education, and given us the luxuries he could afford.

> Of all the things that life can bring,
> I ask but only three-
> Bread for my need,
> Books to read,
> And a house beside the sea.
>
> *Anon.*

Another new emotion was experienced that summer, one to which I was not accustomed, and one which still today causes me problems. That is the dislike (resentment?) of needing to depend on others, especially my children, to assist with chores and problems I can't handle alone. There is a fine line to walk between being independent and accepting help when it is offered and needed. Determined to remain in control of life and its daily dictates, it is difficult for me to accept the role reversal of parent-child. Yet, I constantly tell my daughters it is not they whom I resent, but the circumstances of life which put me in need of their help. Further confusing the issue is the realization I would be devastated should they not be willing to help me in times of need. Constantly I talk to myself about learning to accept help graciously, to allow them the pleasure of being of assistance to their mother.

The same feelings surface when I am issued invitations to join brothers or sisters for their own family occasions. It is loathsome and distasteful to be *included*. The demeaning feeling of being a "third thumb" or a "fifth wheel" is no longer just a cliché. It has become in fact an unwelcome reality. In all honesty I confess that I am totally aware of the kindness and concern which motivate the issuance of the invitations and I am also intensely grateful. I would be despondent if they should *not* invite me! But the sense of being on the outside, a party-crasher, is difficult to conquer. Self-analysis has now become another first-time product of my widowhood!

Beach retreat, Ocean Isle Beach, North Carolina

Chapter 8

Hurricane Fran

September 1996. Hurricane season in North Carolina. Fran had been watched for days as she beat a relentless course toward the Carolinas. Howard's death was only two months behind me.

I had re-discovered my need for the beach condo and now it was being threatened. Mother drove with me to the beach to secure as much as possible of the property there. We stored the outside furniture and placed rolled-up towels on window and door sills. That night as we slept there was no storm, no winds, nothing threatened, all seemed so quiet. As we prepared to leave early the following morning, police with loud speakers rode by the house warning that immediate evacuation of the island was mandatory. We hurriedly removed some treasured pictures from the walls and other small items which had been gifts. My urge to take everything which I could load into the car was controlled by remembering Howard's frequent admonition, "When you buy beach property, expect it to be threatened. Prepare the best you can, keep your insurance paid, and then relax." When we left the island, Mother and I wondered aloud to each other what kind of damage we would discover when we were permitted to return after the storm. Again, I was dealing with a situation which had been experienced before, but always as "we"—Howard and I—not by myself.

Fran spared the beach. Instead, before inflicting too much damage to the coastline, she cut inland and headed directly for Raleigh and Wake County, more than 150 miles northwest! During the afternoon, news broadcasts kept us advised of the probable path and the possibility that landfall might not noticeably diminish the power of the storm. Arriving back in Wake County, I took Mother to her home where she would be alone as would I. We had received storm/hurricane warnings before and the storms always weakened after hitting land and before reaching our part of the state. We did not see need for undue worry. As night approached I checked my candle supply (just in case!) and then continued my normal nightly routine.

Marilyn was working until 11:00 at Wake Medical Center, just a few blocks away. In the early evening she telephoned to be sure I was calm and to tell me her plan should the storm become severe for us. She would come to my house if it became impossible for her to drive the ten miles to her home in Wendell. I still did not anticipate that anything severe would happen, but welcomed her plans. Then the power failed! The storm hit with a vengeance and the noise escalated. In the dark, I could hear sounds of things outside blowing around and falling. At times the house shuddered as though being shaken by a giant hand. Lightning momentarily illuminated the darkness. Thunder and noises roared non-stop and rain fell in torrents. I sat in my chair, listening, not knowing what was happening outside but not daring to move about.

Long after midnight Marilyn arrived and told of a harrowing forty-five minutes trying to drive the half dozen blocks from the hospital. Trees were down and every street was blocked. Power lines dangled in the wind and could be seen at every lightning flash. How grateful I was for her safe arrival, and how grateful I was to have her with me (but guilty that she was not with her husband).

For hours we sat in the den listening to the terror going on outside. Frequently there would be a loud crash and we would breathe again when we realized the house was intact. Occasionally we prowled from room to room, candles in hand, checking ceilings and windows for cracks and leaks. Peering out the back windows when the lightning flashed gave us no hint of the condition of the yard. Rain slanted across our view, obscuring what lay beyond. After seemingly endless hours of pure turmoil, the storm quieted somewhat and we decided to try to nap. Thankfully, we did, and that rest helped prepare us for what we discovered when dawn finally broke.

Our street was blocked by downed trees and power lines. My backyard was covered by fallen pines, and the view of their roots, upturned, loomed before us. Every tree had fallen *away* from the house! Howard's prized fruit trees were uprooted, and the day lilies, of which he had been so proud, were crushed beneath the fallen pines. The door to the outside storage was off its hinges, and power and cable service would not be restored for weeks. Neighbors who rarely saw each other in our busy lives went solemnly from house to house, checking on each other, exclaiming over and over about the total devastation each had suffered. But no person was harmed!

The same picture greeted Mother who had lost huge and ancient oaks from the grove around her house. But our houses and lives were spared, and we were grateful for undamaged roofs. My gratitude was directed to the One who had helped me endure the storm with a degree of calmness, and without total paralyzing fear, even though I was without the comforting presence of my husband. I also uttered prayers of thanksgiving for Marilyn. With highways impassable and with phone service lost, she did not know during the morning hours how her husband and her own house had weathered the storm.

Now the aftermath had to be faced. It was a challenge to secure someone to clear the trees since the whole city was like a fallen forest. Finding money to pay for the job was another problem, for I was still very uneasy about my financial security (or lack thereof!) Once the trees had been removed, I began trying to save the daylilies and the azaleas which had been uprooted with the trees. Shrubs and dogwoods had to be planted and landscape timbers laid in an attempt to preserve the bank on which the pines had grown. The task continues even today, years later. The bank still has not been stabilized, and each storm causes more of it to be washed into the yard. The problems caused by uprooted trees are far from being conquered. And for all these years I've wondered how my husband would have handled the problems which I have been forced to solved—alone.

Another first-time episode occurred during the clean-up process, one which I had never expected to happen, and which today seems humorous but wasn't the least bit humorous as it happened. Since the daylilies were becoming dormant in September, it seemed the best way to save them was to dig the bulbs and replant them in beds and rows which could be kept free of weeds. Shovel and wheelbarrow were the tools for the job. In an effort to locate the bulbs I crawled about, on hands and knees, in the debris left by the fallen trees. One day I looked behind me to the space just cleared and there lay a snake in the very spot where I had worked. He was not black and he was not short! I yelled, "Howa—!" He was not there! When I realized I had reverted to my normal habit of expecting Howard to do the dirty work, I also realized that I must do it now. I had never, ever killed a snake. Pushing down all my abhorrence, I said, "Stay there, snake, while I go get a hoe!" Unbelievably, the animal lay still while I ran to the tool house, found a hoe and returned to chop him apart. Another "first" and a decidedly unpleasant one. Without hesitation I did it, but afterwards there was no one to whom I could boast. In more recent years I have been forced to repeat that experience, once when I nearly stepped on a moccasin on the carport. I killed it, with the same fear and disgust as before. And there still is no one to whom I can boast about my newfound bravery!

*Uprooted trees: Cooke home, Raleigh,
after Hurricane Fran, September 1996*

Chapter 9

Life Must Go On

Those who lose their mates and face life alone are nearly always advised by well-meaning persons that "life must go on," or told, with a note of criticism, to "get on with your life." It's easy to repeat the cliché, but that truly doesn't give the listener much help. Life as it was known before will not be the same again. Everything will change, will be indelibly different. The newly widowed person will seek purpose, not just activity. Questions of identity will be desperately faced, especially by women. For me, it was particularly difficult since I had also just recently retired from the work force. Always, when asked to tell about myself, my answer would begin with my working title and job. Next I was a wife, mother, daughter, etc. Now, having neither job nor husband, I felt that I had lost my identity. I was desperate for some structure to my life, a tangible goal. But what would it be?

First I tried volunteer work. That provided a sense of satisfaction for a while, but as often happens to a willing volunteer, the promised hours of work escalated to full-time, without remuneration. There was no future in it!

My grandchildren who lived nearby filled my need in many ways. I was able to help their busy parents by picking them up from school when needed, taking them to music lessons, etc. I could function as an occasional sitter, but what I really preferred (and what they needed) was just a grandmother, not a permanent caregiver. We were able, however, to do special things together, take trips, go to the beach and the museums, but grandchildren grow up and they could not provide my permanent identity.

It was also possible to fill lots of hours helping my mother, who still lived alone. Other brothers and sisters (nine of them!) shared that activity with me so that would not be the basis for determining what I should do for the rest of my life. Happily, when Mother did require full-time assistance following a fall which resulted in broken limbs, I was the one who was able to provide for her needs. I have happily accepted a role of driving her to keep doctor appointments, to visit graves of her parents and siblings, to the beach, Christmas shopping, lunching, etc. Still, that could not identify me!

Giving more time to church activities was a definite possibility. I agreed once again to serve as a deacon. When asked to accept a three-year term on the church finance committee, I said, "Yes." My Sunday School class needed a teacher and again I accepted the responsibility. Visiting shut-ins and hospitalized church members was added to my activity list. When the church began a fund-raising effort for the relocation project, I was asked to help write some of the publicity material. There was work enough to last a lifetime. But that had been the career work from which I had retired—was that really how I wished to live out my days?

There were, of course, many other options, and as I flitted from one to the other, I had the uneasy feeling that I was simply running about and avoiding the real issue. But what was the issue? I *did* know, however, that the choices needed to be mine, not those which someone else thought would be good for me. And I also knew I must prove to myself that I could, as always before, manage somehow to regulate my days and make my choices. Still, without any clear leading, life just went on from one day to the next, from one routine to another, without definite purpose.

Four generations travel to New York
Left to right: Anita, Angela, Frances, Mother Lewis

Chapter 10

Solace on the Road

During that first summer, I drove from North Carolina to central Pennsylvania to visit Anita's family. The grandsons had spent a week with me, and when it was time for them to go home, I volunteered (eagerly!) to take them. Driving the distance, with no other driver along, was a return to a familiar way of life and I relished it. Then, as Thanksgiving approached, it was decided that we should observe it together as we usually did, but this year we would gather in Pennsylvania, requiring another drive by me.

Thanksgiving was Howard's favorite, his *special* holiday. As a born-and-bred Massachusetts "pilgrim" (which I always teasingly called him), Thanksgiving had to be observed according to the traditions which his family had followed. It was a big day for them, and was always observed with the same sense of importance by us. Our children grew up with that tradition. In more recent years, Marilyn's family responsibilities were directed to Grady's parents, but Anita and her family would often join her father and me at the beach. There we cooked all the traditional foods and ate together in a wonderful spirit of gratitude and "life is fun and good." There was always time for the grandchildren to gather on the beach to feed the gulls their Thanksgiving feast of left-overs.

Now, however, this year would be terribly different. Going to State College, Pennsylvania to visit them would be a clean break with prior customs. My mother accepted our invitation to share the holiday with us and to travel with me. We anticipated the holiday with excitement—and with pain. There was a great deal of both. The unexpected minor deterrents began immediately. On our arrival in the city, the fog was so thick I could not read street signs. A photo of Howard and me in the living room kept me elsewhere in the house. Preparing all the traditional food was familiar, enjoyable, and bittersweet. Prayer around the table was so difficult. But the trip was wonderful, and we now call it the most enjoyable/difficult of any holiday in recent years. It was brightened by a beautiful snow and the never-to-be-forgotten scene of Steve grilling turkey on the deck in the snow! We drove home in snow and rain. I had proven I could do it still! Surely this qualified as getting on with life.

There were still other places to which I was yearning to return, and ultimately I did go back to many of them. First was the need to go home—Howard's home. I was homesick for it. A family wedding made it an easy decision, and with two grandchildren with me, the drive was again a testing time. No problem! It was on this trip that I dared to drive up Mt. Washington in New Hampshire, something Howard had always refused to do. Adam's begging challenged me and I couldn't let him down! The real testing, however, came as I saw Howard's hometown, visited his family, and returned to the familiar streets and places without him.

Now that I was on the road again, other trips followed in rapid succession. New York City had always been a regular stop-over on our treks to and from Massachusetts. Together, we enjoyed the Broadway theater, dinners in popular restaurants, shopping and just the excitement and variety of the big city. Dare I try it without Howard? Did I even *want* to go without him? The decision was easily made when Anita, Angela and I decided to take my mother for a Broadway week-end. We hit the town non-stop, and filled every minute with activity. We even attracted attention in blasé New York as waiters and sales people marveled at the vitality and youthfulness of my 95-year old mother and at the unusual scene of four generations traveling and playing together.

Two months later my yearning for Amherst dominated my thoughts again. It was "leaf season" in the Berkshires. What better excuse did I need? When I informed my daughters, I sensed their disapproval of my plan to drive. I admitted my car did have an excess number of miles on it. Reluctantly I faced the truth that perhaps the girls had a legitimate concern when they reminded me of the dangers for a woman alone on such a trip—especially a woman of my age! The issue of age had never occurred to me except casually, but now I did need to consider it. Still unwilling to give in completely to every caution that was raised, I compromised. I flew to Newburgh, N.Y., up the river from New York City, rented a car there and drove the remaining distance to Amherst. What did I prove to myself? In all honesty, the obvious proof was that my desire for independence, and to be able to make my own decisions, had not died when Howard did. I did admit to myself, however, that my children were rightfully cautious to express concern. And I further admitted, secretly to myself, that my determination for independence caused me to sometimes throw caution to the wind.

One summer weekend David and I, just the two of us, went to the Outer Banks of North Carolina. I felt he needed some special attention from Grandmother. It was the summer the Hatteras lighthouse had just been moved and the production of *The Lost Colony* was still playing. Neither his brother nor sister had ever been to this part of the state, and it would be a special treat for him to have the first opportunity. It worked! We had an educational as well as entertaining trip, and one which was so very satisfying to me.

My traveling obsession had really begun several months prior to the events just described. During Howard's illness we had kept in touch with friends who lived in England, Scotland and Sweden. Even then I knew that someday I would feel a compulsion to visit them. They were mourning with me, long distance, and my heart needed the personal sharing with friends of our mutual sorrow. Too, I was not yet prepared to give up every opportunity to travel to Europe. Howard and I had grown to have great affection for so much of it and there was still too much to see. But could I manage it alone? I had to discover if it were still a possibility for me.

In the first months when I had begun to openly talk about making a European trip, Anita casually(?) suggested that sometime I take a grandchild on such a journey. She had been to Europe while in college, and continued to have wandering feet, a trait she and Steve were instilling in their family. Whether her motive was to give a travel experience to one of her children, or whether it was suggested as a safety measure for me, I've never ascertained.

Whatever her reasoning, Adam, then fifteen years old, became my travel companion, a plan I happily promoted. It was a perfect arrangement. Adam was a knowledgeable young man with a keen mind. His manners were impeccable and his personality exuded calmness and self-assurance. Our relationship had always been one of love and respect between grandmother and grandson, and the two weeks traveling together did not destroy that. My joy was to show him all the things tourists should see, which were already familiar to me. He quickly learned how to find our way on the subway and the trains, and I delighted in introducing him to my friends. And, as was his custom, he would often "con" me into securing reservations at the most expensive restaurants in London, Edinburgh and all places in between. The trip affirmed for me, once and for all, that I can go wherever I wish, as long as I can find the money!

In retrospect, I now understand that it was necessary for me to put all these trips behind me as part of learning who I was and what I was to do with life. At the time, however, I simply felt compelled to face them, to test myself. As time passes, I continue to enjoy travel, but I had to first learn if it was truly an option for me—alone.

Travels with Adam,
Stonehenge in England

Chapter 11

Defining Independence

Two weeks following our return from England, I became ill. This was not the first illness since Howard's death, illness being a circumstance I had feared and dreaded, but it was the first without obvious cause. Previously, following hurricane Fran, while working in the remains of the fallen trees, I had contracted poison ivy. Waking at two o'clock in the morning and finding one eye completely shut, I knew the *reason* for the swelling and pain. Since there was no one to give me a second opinion about the course of action I should take, I decided I must seek help immediately, before both eyes should become infected, causing total blindness. So, I drove myself at two a.m., with one good eye, across town to the Rex Hospital emergency room. There had been other episodes of illness, including bronchitis and cataract surgery, but they were labeled minor inconveniences, and, with help of my children, they were quickly dealt with.

This current illness, however, promised to be no short-term inconvenience. It began with excruciating headaches and, having experienced a cerebral aneurysm, my fear now was that this signaled neurological problems. C-scans were ordered, twice. (Diagnosis following one was meningitis!) Another diagnosis was depression, but prescription medication did not help. My vision became blurred and distorted. Driving became impossible, and I made several visits to the ophthalmologist, driven there by helpful neighbors. Further results were all negative, but still the illness persisted and increased in intensity. Months passed. I knew my body well enough to realize something was definitely wrong. How I missed Howard! Frightened and unable to go on with a normal life, it was devastating to face each day alone.

My doctor said to me, and to Marilyn, that he did not know what else to do to find the cause! Of one thing I was certain, I could not continue in that state of health. I tearfully told myself that my husband would have had a solution. He would have found help, somewhere, someway. By this time I was truly depressed simply because I felt so helplessly frustrated.

Anita insisted she knew of a wonderful doctor and diagnostician at Duke Hospital and she would be able to secure an appointment with him immediately. Marilyn, still nursing at Wake Med, eagerly concurred. It was a life-saving decision. The doctor at Duke approached the problem from a new and different perspective, tests and biopsies were quickly performed, medication was prescribed, and I was given almost instant relief from the six-month ordeal. How wonderful! Later, when my primary care doctor asked who had referred me to Duke, I happily replied, "My daughters!"

The time had now come for consideration of major changes in my lifestyle. That illness made me have great sympathy for the thousands of other persons living alone with their illnesses, not knowing where to turn. I also began to examine my own situation with more objectivity. Perhaps the time was approaching, sooner than I had hoped, when I should dispose of some of my responsibilities, such as house and large yard, and think seriously about moving. While the possibility of such a change had occurred to me previously, now I gave it serious consideration. Independence, I realized, was not just about having my own stubborn way about everything. True independence entailed making decisions with wisdom and knowledge. It would only come when I, voluntarily, recognized the necessity of giving up some of my so-called independence and made some serious decisions about my future, by myself, while I had the faculties to do so. Just living alone in my house would surely be no indication of independence if it became necessary for my children to run errands for me, take me to the doctor and to church, monitor my medications, and feel they must care for my needs on a daily basis. Now I knew that such an existence could in no way be called "independence." Yet, I still was not prepared to give up completely the kind of life I had enjoyed with my life companion. Widowed persons are advised to not make hurried decisions such as selling a homestead and moving to a new location. I still clung to that advice. I would need to give a little more thought and time to that idea!

Finally, nearly five years after Howard's death, I took the major step of putting my house on the market. Never before had I attempted such a large task about which I knew so little. Previously, when we had bought and sold other property, the only involvement required of me was my signature on the numerous documents. Howard had done all the work and I had not questioned the procedures. Now I began to read newspaper and magazine articles. Questions were posed to family members who had often been involved in real estate transfers. There was a necessity to familiarize myself, somewhat, with the terms and language to be encountered. Otherwise I would feel myself to be completely stupid and vulnerable.

A year later the house had not been sold. Some mistakes were made along the way. Once again I recalled that, even as a team, my husband and I had also made mistakes. Once again I recalled his admonition to do the best of which I was capable and then not stay awake at night worrying about the failures. Still there remains the need and the desire to dispose of the house and the burden and expense of its upkeep. There are so many things which I prefer doing rather than caring for house and yard. Now, too, I am beginning to sense the emotional need to make a change of residence. Howard is not here. New surroundings may be called for.

Chapter 12

Regrets and Failures

When naming all the things I have been forced to do for the first time, I realize there are some experiences I have been spared. Friends tell of their despair and tears caused by the desolate feeling of the empty bed. Not once have I felt that loneliness. Perhaps the weeks when Howard was hospitalized, or the months when he used a hospital bed at home, helped me become accustomed to his absence from our bed. Whatever the reason, I am grateful for the lack of that traumatic emotion. Neither have I been bothered by dreams while sleeping, which others tell me cause them great anguish. Actually, it was months after his death before I had a first dream of him and I was beginning to feel cheated! Now, when I do have sleep dreams that include him, they always replay some normal part of our lives which may have passed through my mind during the day without my taking notice.

There are, however, hundreds of little happenings that I want to share with him. As the years since his death increase, those times of missing his presence don't seem to lessen. Today I watched workmen remove a tall power pole and replace it with an even taller one. The equipment was massive and the work to avoid other power lines, as well as dwellings, looked daunting to me. Howard would have given me a play-by-play account and explanation of what was being done and how easy it all would be. How I missed him!

Every full moon is a personal attack on my heart. Whatever is romantic about the full moon struck him the first time he visited me at my home before we married. We sat on the front porch, with the moon above in all its splendor, while Howard serenaded me with "Carolina moon, shine upon the one I love." And I didn't know he could sing! Thereafter, whenever the moon shone brightly, whether full or not, we always laughed and remembered those wonderful first days of our attraction for each other. I still do!

I turn to him to exclaim about a beautiful sunset or a shooting star. Meteor showers bring back the memories of the times we drove to Quabbin Reservoir to observe, away from city lights, an August display of meteors. Or the night we walked the beach with our oldest grandson, Ivan, and his friend and counted the shooting stars by the dozens.

The smell of his brand of smoking tobacco can bring me to my knees when I start to speak and realize the someone smoking nearby is not my husband. I walk the beach and look up to see a man standing with his knees locked and his hands on his hips and for an instant feel joy because Howard is meeting me as usual—only it is someone else.

When I drive through our town, I want to share with him the wonder of all the changes. He would have known beforehand about every new street to be built or every new housing development. I am crushed when there is no one with whom to exclaim about the endless construction going on. Events on the news every night at dinnertime lose their significance without Howard to make an observation about the happenings.

Frequently I am awakened from sleep by a sound like that of his chair creaking in the den. Other nights I hear his footsteps in the hallway as though he were walking to the bedroom.

I weep that he is missing the joy of watching our grandchildren grow to adulthood. I attend school concerts, graduations, birthday celebrations, recitals, weddings—and then go home wishing I could relive each exciting moment with my husband. The nursing school graduation ceremony of Christy, our first granddaughter, was especially bittersweet, for he would have exulted in that victory for her. His pride in each of their accomplishments would have been as great as mine, and I want to talk to him about it.

Recently my pastor and I were having a quiet discussion about these feelings of mine, and I said to him, "I don't think I will ever get over missing him." To which Mark replied, "I don't think you are supposed to!" When I feel that I harbor an unhealthy hold on the past, I am freed by Mark's comment.

There have been some regrets for the times I failed as a companion. My acceptance of the past as being beyond recall keeps me fairly stable emotionally. But still my guilt does intrude on my peace. Howard liked to surprise me with small appliances for the kitchen, and I often thought they were unnecessary. It was difficult to express honest gratitude! He enjoyed playing cards and board games. They bored me. Refusal to join the game was more gracious on my part than being a pouting player, I reasoned, but even then I felt guilty. He was a skater, and not once did I ever try skating with him. He enjoyed bowling and for a time played on his company team. I never attended nor watched him bowl a single game. He was a better dancer than I, and although I did try that a few times, I was always less than accomplished at it. Today I pray that he knew that I loved him and respected his different interests. I pray that he forgave my frequent failures to be the compliant partner.

An item in the recent news caught my attention. Benedict Carey of the *L.A. Times* reported on experiments conducted by researchers studying happy marriages. When they analyzed the changes in the well-being of recently divorced or widowed persons, they were astonished to discover that what they had expected to find was not the reality. They had anticipated that people with "high levels of life satisfaction would have the resources to buffer themselves against life's cruelties." Those persons who had been able to deal with tragedies in the family, with job and career disappointments, and other dramatic life changes were expected to do the same after divorce or death of a mate. Just the opposite was true. "Those whose lives had been the most satisfactory, those who had been able to bounce back from all other adversities with their internal good cheer intact, plunged most deeply after the death of a spouse," they wrote. Researchers reported that those persons often required an average of eight years to regain their previous level of well being. They concluded, "The person who is very satisfied with life because marriage is wonderful simply has more to lose if his or her spouse dies!" (From *The News & Observer*, March 25, 2003). After reading that, I decided I would not feel guilty again when I continue to miss my husband in all the little occurrences of life.

Howard in Tsingtao, China
December 1945

Howard, wearing his field jacket,
on the drill field (now a ball field) in Tsingtao

Chapter 13

Advancing to Fulfillment

Winter of the year 2000–2001 was difficult. I denied the existence of depression, but secretly I suspected it was becoming a reality for me. I had no goals, nothing for which to aim, no purpose in life. There were dozens of things I could do, but none were challenging. Everything seemed so monotonous and so repetitious, just more of the same weary tedium. I paced by day and lay awake at night, questioning and pleading with God to answer the question I kept asking Him, "What am I supposed to do with the rest of my life?"

In desperation I gradually began to receive and formulate some resolutions to the question. I decided then to sell the house, to move to something smaller which required less upkeep. Saving money on expenses, repairs and yard work surely would contribute to a happier outlook for me. With a vengeance I began to plan, to organize in my mind the process of disposing of fifty years' worth of accumulated "things." The logical place to begin was to clear out closets, cabinets, and drawers and use the winter months to systematically sort the treasures from the trash. My plan was to accomplish much of that part of the job before the spring months arrived, when I would put up a "For Sale" sign.

While collecting my thoughts about the project, and stalling about beginning it, I learned that my college freshman grandson, Adam, would possibly request my help in writing a paper he had been assigned at Wake Forest University. It required first-hand information about World War II from someone who had been involved. Adam, knowing that his grandfather had written letters to me from the Pacific area during that conflict, wondered to his mother if I might give him access to those letters. Being unaccustomed to denying him anything I could conceivably supply, I agreed. But first I needed to read those letters! They were, after all, very personal. Most of them had passed between Howard and me during the year he was stationed as a Marine in the Pacific and in China. They had not been read since his return to the United States in 1946, and I felt they might need to be censored before a grandson read them. The footlocker where they were stored would be the first object of my house cleaning project.

Clearing closets and drawers strikes a death blow to every time-frame one sets for accomplishing such a task. For me, that one chest ended all possibilities that I might ever finish the job. It was a relic, a treasured memento. The footlocker had been with Howard all through his service in the Marine Corps. For years we had used it to store items which we wanted as keepsakes, and beginning my cleaning chore with it was a big mistake! Every picture, every newspaper item, all the cards and letters, travel folders, even old grade books from my teaching years—all were cause for study and inspection, and consumed days to examine.

In the bottom of the chest were the letters, more than 200 of them. Letters which Howard and I had written to each other from the time we met. Every letter he received from me while he was in China had been brought home, and I had saved all that he had written to me. They had been in that chest for more than fifty years! I read—and read—and cried—and laughed—and remembered—and realized I had also forgotten a lot! In his letters were maps, Chinese paper money from 1945-46, and items clipped from the military newspaper.

Every letter had to be read. When I had initially received them, I must have read only the "I love you" parts, for now I was learning about his life in that foreign environment as if it were the first time. There were many comments such as, "I'll tell you more about it when I am home." He never did, and we never looked at them together. They were stored away and forgotten as we went on with our busy lives after he was discharged from the Marines. Through the years he had told me about the city where he was stationed and about Tsingtao University where he had lived. He had related to our daughters some instances of hearing guns as the Communists began to move down from the north of China. And when we had begun to have opportunity to travel, he had often remarked that he would like to take me to Tsingtao, but China was not open to tourists in those years. The letters were a treasure-trove and I cherished them as though they were freshly written. I had no idea what I would do with them, but I knew I must keep them for my daughters to read someday after I am gone!

Now, as I look back on what happened for me in the next days and months, I know it was all providential. At the time, of course, I had not the hindsight which now allows me to see that none of the events were merely coincidental. God was answering my prayer, my plea for putting some purpose in my days. I will never again doubt that He cares about even the little things that affect us.

Hardly had I begun sorting through the letters when I happened to read an item in the news which caused me to gasp. It was a request for volunteer teachers of conversational English in China! Details were given of the need in the upcoming university summer sessions, and specifically mentioned Qingdao (formerly Tsingtao) University. That was "our" city, "our" university. Rarely had I ever heard the city mentioned in prior years and I could hardly believe what I was reading. The contact person was CP (name not given for sake of privacy), a man with whom I was acquainted through my work, and application had to be made to him. Dare I consider such a thing? Did I qualify? Could I handle the expense? "No," I said to myself. But the idea would not die. I debated, procrastinated, considered and reconsidered. Then, as the deadline approached, I knew I must at least investigate the possibility.

When the application arrived from the sponsoring company, I realized my qualifications met all their requirements, except my age was just over the limit. A health statement erased their doubts, and I secured the required recommendations while CP stayed in touch and encouraged me. As the process moved forward, I realized the application did not guarantee a position in Qingdao and that I could possibly be sent to one of a dozen Chinese universities. Wanting this to be a true voluntary mission effort, I did not mention my interest in Qingdao and was willing to go wherever I might be sent. When all details were completed and I had been accepted, I then broke my silence and told friends and family, including my 95-year old mother, who happily encouraged me despite the fears we both were harboring.

The spring was a busy time. I had suddenly gone from asking what I was to do with my life to the point of there being insufficient time to accomplish all that now stared me in the face. My house was now in the hands of the realtor and was being shown to prospects. I was receiving instructions and lesson plans daily from the company in Hong Kong, and friends and family were helping me collect (and pay for) all the teaching aids I would need to take with me. And then I received my assignment. It was Changsha, hundreds of miles south-west of Qingdao!

I was disappointed but not discouraged. My prayers for direction in life were being answered in a remarkable way and I dared not complain that I could not have complete control of the plan. In briefing meetings with CP and others of the North Carolina team, we learned that all except six of us would go to Qingdao. Finally, I shared with the group my personal interest in Qingdao and asked them to take lots of pictures to share with me when the summer was over.

The experience in Changsha was a once-in-a-lifetime happening. My class was composed of thirty students—polite, eager, accomplished and teachable. Many became e-mail friends. Our team of six teachers struggled with problems of food, language, transportation, heat, and the constant duty required of us by the university. All of us had expected to have some free time for travel. Ann (not her real name), the youngest in our group and a single mom, was especially disappointed, and vociferous about our inability to see the Great Wall. We were too far away to travel in the spare time we were granted. The group leader, a company employee who lived in Changsha, hoped to be transferred farther north. When told about my interest in Qingdao (by Ann, not by me!) she tried to arrange an appointment for herself there, and insisted that I make travel plans to accompany her to Qingdao. That, too, failed to happen. It would have been a quick trip, I had no idea what I would do or see in a short time, and I did not wish to impose myself on the team which was teaching there. I was truly relieved when those plans failed.

At the end of the summer, the teams gathered again in Hong Kong, and CP informed me that I *would* be included in his team the following summer. He had a personal invitation from the dean to return with twenty teachers and he expected me to go. My response was, "Maybe." September 11 occurred shortly after our return which made travel plans for a year hence seem daunting. My house was still on the market and money was in short supply. CP stayed in touch all year, however, and I did return to China in 2002, to Qingdao, to teach in the very university where my husband had lived more than fifty years earlier.

As we approached the Qingdao airport, the teachers shared my excitement as I saw the city for the first time. They felt they were part of the miracle which I knew was taking place. They kept telling me, however, that the old university buildings had been razed and all new structures had been erected. But when I saw the location of the school, in a new part of the city, I knew this was not the area where Howard had been stationed. I immediately began asking questions. First, the dean assured me that the old campus was in the old part of town and the buildings were now used as another school. Three other persons confirmed his information. One of our high school students assured me the dean was correct, for he, too, knew where the old school was located. Another was a young Communist businessman who was my partner for a university-sponsored visit to a privately owned manufacturing company some distance out of the city. He wrote instructions and the address for me so that I might give them to a taxi driver if I wished to find the school.

Our weekends were free time for us, unlike the previous summer. The teachers had planned excursions for Xian, the site of the famed terracotta soldiers, and for the Great Wall. I had prepared for both trips by having sufficient funds; our first trip was to be to Beijing and from there to the Great Wall. I was excited and was especially happy for Ann, who was in our team this year and who had wanted so badly to see the Great Wall in the prior year. Just before the planned weekend, I overheard someone remark that Ann had not signed on to go. I was distressed and after cautious questioning, and finally being brave enough to talk to Ann herself about it, I learned that it was a lack of money for her, a problem which I had suspected. I knew I could never go and enjoy the sightseeing if Ann should be left behind. She reluctantly agreed to allow my roommate and me to pay her way. That meant, of course, that I would not have funds to go on the next excursion to Xian. My generosity was not always that natural with me, and later I knew that it was providential that I shared with her.

The president of the sponsoring company for teachers was a Chinese-American. His wife, Roby, was a North Carolinian. During the week before the planned trip to Xian, the women of the teaching team were invited for dessert at their apartment one evening. It was a delightful social hour as we shared with them our impressions of China and why we felt led to volunteer for the work, and to hear of their lives and the work they led. Ann, always the talker, told Roby of my longtime knowledge of Qingdao because my husband had been stationed there. She went on to tell her that Ann and I would be alone on campus the following weekend as the other team members traveled to Xian, and that we were planning to spend our time searching for the old university where my husband had lived. Roby immediately expressed excitement and a desire to go with us.

Wonderful! She spoke the language and she knew her way about town. We eagerly included her in our plans, and on Saturday morning she met us at the taxi stand. I gave her the address given to me earlier by the Communist businessman and she took over from there, talking with the driver and excitedly telling him why we were making the search. He acknowledged the address was very familiar to him. Roby told us her tutor, a dear Chinese friend, might live near our destination. The taxi driver confirmed the address was across the street. Could any of this be labeled "coincidence"?

When the taxi stopped at the gate, there was no doubt in my mind this was truly the old Tsingtao University. Through the trees I could see the roof of the main building, so familiar, just as Howard had described it. I was overcome with emotion and I would have been content to end the search right there. I had at last made connection with Howard and the whole year of our lives which had been lost to us fifty-seven years earlier. I cried.

Ann and Roby were in tears with me. Then Roby recognized, across the street, the apartment of her friend, Rachel, and wanted us to go meet the family. We were welcomed so warmly into their very small apartment, and Rachel agreed to go with us onto the university campus. Now there were two people with me who could speak the language.

The main building was old, with a wide circular staircase. I had heard about that stairway before! The windows looked out back on a narrow courtyard, and beyond were other buildings in a square, all with red tile roofs of the German tradition. I had heard about those roofs! We walked across campus. Because Howard had written to me that he was moving to a special building, Roby and Rachel were able to talk to people we met about such a building which might have once housed foreign occupation forces. I was in a state of virtual unbelief as we wandered. There, off to my left, was a soccer field. Without doubt it had been the drill field for Howard and his men. I had a picture in my wallet to prove it.

And then, around the corner, we found the building, with a plaque on the wall by the door giving information about American soldiers who had lived there in 1945! Unbelievable! My husband had walked through that very door—on those steps—down this street—before me. I knew, without doubt, that God had allowed me to have this unexpected and undeserved experience. He had led every step of the way, beginning with the previous year when the trip from Changsha to Qingdao was impossible. I had to wait for God's time, which was obviously not the year before. He was there when I was generous with Ann and helped make it possible for her to realize her dream of seeing the Great Wall. He was there when I was told by four different persons that I rightly recognized the new Qingdao University buildings were not on the location of the old. He was there when Roby expressed a desire to go with us that Saturday, and He was there when Rachel, who could talk and ask questions in Chinese, accompanied us on our walk around the university grounds. It would have been impossible for me to ever have planned this experience so perfectly. Only God could have made it happen.

Later, in my room, and still overcome by the enormity of what I had felt, I put my thoughts in a letter to Howard.

Qingdao (Tsingtao), China
July 2002

Oh, my love,

You are supposed to be here with me. Why being in this place should be a homecoming to me is still a mystery. It was so long ago that you were here, when you had left me behind, that it is difficult to explain why I felt so possessive of this place. It is your town, our town, and the letters we exchanged have come alive for me. I yearn desperately for your physical presence here. Surely I did not come seeking that! I'm alone. Dear God, someday, someday let your promises come true.

On this Saturday the Lord led the way. Without question, He led in every step. To have Roby volunteer eagerly to go with Anne and me seeking where you, love, had lived was not even the first sign the Lord was leading. Already four different persons here have told me where old Tsingtao University was located. One of them, a young Chinese man who had been my "partner" on a bus trip to a local factory, had written the address of the university in my book. It was confirmed for me that the university where you lived was not this new, modern university where I am teaching. Roby met Anne and me at the gate. She gave the taxi driver the address, which he immediately acknowledged without hesitation. Then Roby said her friend, her tutor, Chinese Rachel, lived across the street from the university, at least she thought so.

The cab pulled into the gated entrance of the university, and there in front of me was a beautiful old building, just as I had imagined. And there, directly across the street, was Rachel's house. Roby took us there to see if Rachel would like to go with us into the university grounds. We met Rachel's lovely family—her husband who works for ABI, Inc., her baby daughter Rebecca, her in-laws who were visiting from New York, and a sister—6 people living in two rooms with a total size of my kitchen in the States. Gracious lovely people. My day could have been complete even at this point. Rachel did accompany us to the university. We entered the main building. It was old, dark, had beautiful staircases, and could easily have been a home for occupying Marines. But there were many buildings. How to know where you, love, had lived was not possible. We walked past a rose garden. We noted dates when buildings had been erected, all before 1945. We noted the layout of the buildings and their construction, which was of stone and brick as you had described. The trees growing on this beautiful campus were certainly alive more than fifty years ago. We went by a ball field, a playground—and there it was! Your drill field where you had told me your men drilled, at your instruction, just to keep them busy and not bored! The picture of you in field jacket must have been taken at that very place!

We continued our stroll, exploring, in our minds imagining where you had been. Then Rachel talked to a man on campus, who obviously worked there, and he immediately told her of a building with plaques telling of American soldiers living there. We had already taken a side street, and had taken a picture of me beside one of those buildings, just because it "might be." Rounding to the front, there, on the wall beside the door, was the plaque telling of Americans living in that building in 1945. And it was just down a short distance from the drill field, which was still in sight. We were awe-struck! Tears of joy and bitterness mixed. I would have been content to take a picture at the front gate, but God gave me so much more. More than I could ever have imagined, more than ever crossed my mind.

Roby and Ann and Rachel shared the moments with me in the same feeling of awe I experienced. Our daughters will now have, as will I, some tangible sense of where you were during that year of separation from me. If only you could have brought me here yourself! But I thank God for the miracle that unfolded before me this Saturday.

With all my love forever,
Your Wife.

Frances at door of university building
where Howard had been stationed, Tsingtao, China

Front gate of Tsingtao University

University buildings (note roofs in German tradition)

Roby's friend, Rachel, and her family, Quingdao

Frances at ball field (formerly a drill field in 1945–46)

Golden Wedding celebration, August 25, 1994
Frances and Howard surrounded by their five grandchildren
Back row: Ivan and Christy Harper
Front row: Twins Angela and David Stallings, Adam Stallings

Chapter 14

In the Future

Recovery? Partial. Going on with life? Eagerly. Still believe in God's promises? Definitely.

On His promises I live as one with much hope!

Upon returning to North Carolina, I was immediately faced, again, with an experience that always causes me pain. It is distressing to return home from a wonderful trip but realize the house is empty. No one is there to whom I can tell all the exciting details. (Anita, who had met me at the airport and took me home, did stay with me for a while and let me talk and talk, and I will always be grateful that she understood I needed that.) However, I was granted many opportunities to share my China experiences with Sunday School classes, mission groups, and even grade school classes. Without exception, listeners were amazed at the almost unbelievable experiences and the drama of what I had received. There was no need to embellish or exaggerate any incident. The truth was far more exciting and miraculous than any fiction I could have invented. Of all the foreign operations in which the American military had participated during World War II, many of which had been revisited by some and/or by their families, China was probably the least likely to receive any of those return visits. I felt especially fortunate to have had the incomparable experience of being in that country, in the very city where Howard had been stationed. Whatever I may attempt to do in the years ahead, it will be done with gratitude, for I will always be aware of God's leading and His care.

Each day, alone, I truly become stronger in faith. I find that I make hard decisions with greater ease. Best of all, I've finally begun to learn patience, much of it from Howard's example, and I know, even among my tears, that I am not truly alone. God has proven over and over that He is with me constantly. I am alone, without Howard, but not truly alone as long as I keep faith in God.

Amputees, who are healthy otherwise, usually learn to function without the missing limb. They must participate in many forms of therapy and rehabilitation under the guidance of their physician. I, too, am learning to function without my missing partner. It will require a constant, lifetime effort, and it will necessitate my daily visits to the Great Physician for instruction, guidance and assurance.

[A note from the publisher: This book was originally published by the Mount Olive College Press. In appreciation for their cooperation, we include this essay from the original edition.]

MY RELATIONSHIP WITH MOUNT OLIVE COLLEGE

At the ripe old age of nearly four score years, I have resorted to a great deal of self-analysis. Who and what influenced my life so that I became who I am? Whereas each of us possesses characteristics that are unique to us, still the age-old puzzle of environment versus heredity is reduced to an easy answer: in my case, both were influential. So it was in my life when my church life centered around a Baptist denomination.

Both parents were Baptists, one Southern Baptist, one Free Will Baptist. As a child of the Great Depression, and a farmer's daughter, we usually attended the Baptist church nearest to where we lived at the time. In Pamlico County, we attended the Arapahoe Free Will Baptist Church. Most often we were located nearer Southern Baptist churches, and we attended them. When I reached the age of "accountability," our farm family had no automobile and I rode to the nearest Southern Baptist Church with a kind neighbor with a car. It was there I made my profession of faith at age twelve and which set the pattern for church attendance in adult life.

There was also another strong influence for me. My maternal grandfather was the Reverend John W. Alford, a well-known Free Will Baptist minister. "Dad Alford" was loved and respected by his grandchildren. He was fun to be with and we delighted in visits with him and Mother Alford (Lucy). One of my earliest memories is a visit with him to

Stacy, N.C. where he was to preach on Sunday. A member of the church took us on a BIG BOAT, across the sound to an ISLAND! It was an eye-opening experience for a child of four. Dad Alford was a frequent visitor in our home and I know my love of flying came from him. We lived near Raleigh and on his Sunday afternoon trips to see us, he piled all the children into his car and we went to Raleigh Municipal Airport to watch the Eastern Airline passenger plane land! He knew its scheduled landing time.

As I grew older, I became aware of his role as a preacher and a denominational worker. I had opportunities to hear him preach and to talk about happenings in the churches. When Mount Olive College was born, I was keenly aware of his dream for it and his leadership role in its birth. From the beginning, its first president, Burkett Raper, was known to us as Dad Alford's "son in the ministry." We watched the college grow and prosper into the kind of school he dreamed about. While the Alford family members were not wealthy monetarily, a small memorial endowment was begun at his death, and is still supported by some family members.

At his death in 1960, I was given (inherited) a packet of his sermon outlines. They were written on the backs of envelopes, on grocery lists, on letters to and from friends in the ministry, and were tied with a string. After slipping two of the outlines from the packet (to give to my two daughters as mementos of their great-grandfather), I knew the place for them was in the history collection at Mount Olive College.

I have continued to receive publications from the college and always look for familiar names. Jean Ackiss was introduced to me by Dr. Raper when she was just beginning the program of dinners in the churches, and I have followed the success story of that venture with great appreciation for what has been accomplished through them. I have brought my Mother, Bessie, the last surviving child of John and Lucy Alford and now nearing her 102nd birthday, to the college for special observances. Our family often uses the John and Lucy Alford Endowment fund as the vehicle for gifts at times of death of their descendants and in lieu of Christmas gifts to siblings. Mount Olive College is a special place to our family and has a special place in our respective memories.

Printed in the United States
98250LV00002B/1-9/A